The Book of Lost Recipes

COMPILED BY

Vanessa Kittle

e.s.p. press

Copyright © 2019 By Vanessa Kittle
All Rights Reserved

This book is unofficial and unauthorized.
It is not authorized, approved, or licensed
by the estate of J.R.R. Tolkien or any other entity.

e 10 9 8 7 6 5 4 3 2 1

Foreword

I found this manuscript in the pantry at the old place. It was hidden, or had fallen behind the shelf where we stored the flour and other dry goods. The manuscript appears unfinished, and to be the only copy. I feel it is a terrible shame that these notes weren't included in the great book of our time, because it is obvious how much work was put into them. I feel honor bound to set the record straight and include this, at least in some fashion, into the larger history of our people.

e.fb. 1487

Part 1. Recipes from the tales of The Halfling

Buttery Tea-cakes and Two Beautiful Round Seed-cakes

Our first recipes come from the adventures of the halfling.

Imagine you have enjoyed a quiet morning, followed by a quiet afternoon. Luncheon is long past and you are starting to think of what to have for tea. What would be perfect? Ah, tea-cakes of course, then perhaps a seed-cake or two later. But then there is a loud knock on the door. Oh dear, you remember, you invited that bothersome wizard to tea. It must be him now. No, there's a dwarf standing on your doorstep instead! Well, you have to give him something to eat and drink. It would be terribly rude not to, so you offer him tea, along with some of the delicious tea-cakes you had prepared for your very own meal.

Now there's another knock on the door. The wizard? No, another dwarf. This one is even more venerable than the last. And he is asking for seed-cake. How did he guess that you baked those lovely seed-cakes that afternoon for your after-supper treat? Sadly you know your duty and hurry off to one of your pantries to fetch them, along with some beer from the cellar.

Two dwarves do not a party make. Let's hope no more visitors arrive, you think, but you have an ominous feeling that your larder and pantry are about to be stretched thin.

Two Beautiful Round Seed-cakes

3 cups flour
2 cups wheat flour
2 packets of yeast
¼ cup Ale at room temperature
¼ tsp. salt
6 oz. (1 and ½ sticks) sweet butter
1 and ½ cups sugar
4 eggs, beaten
2 tablespoons seeds (crushed anise, caraway, or cardamom – choose your favorite)
1 and ½ to 2 cups milk

Sift the flour and salt together into a large bowl. Dissolve the yeast in the ale, along with a tablespoon of the sugar. Cream the butter and sugar together in a separate bowl. Beat in the eggs and seeds. Make a well in the flour and add the dissolved yeast. Fold the flour into the yeast mixture, then fold in the butter, sugar and eggs. Slowly beat in enough milk to make a smooth, thick batter. Pour the batter into two 8 inch round greased cake pans. Bake in the middle of your oven at 350° F for 45 minutes, or until a toothpick inserted in the center comes out clean. Let the cakes cool slightly before turning onto a cake rack.

Buttery Tea-cakes
(for 6, including the host!)

1 and ½ cups flour
½ cup butter
½ cup sugar
½ cup dried currants
½ teaspoon salt
1 egg
2 teaspoons baking powder
2 tablespoons milk
Granulated sugar

Sift the flour, sugar, salt, and baking powder together into a large bowl. Work the butter in with your fingertips. Beat the egg and milk, reserving a tablespoon of the egg to glaze the cakes. Mix the wet and dry ingredients together. Roll the dough with your hands into balls the size of a large walnut.

Set the balls on a buttered baking sheet, some distance apart. Brush with the egg wash. Dredge with sugar, and bake at 375 degrees for 12 to 15 minutes, or until lightly golden at the edges.

Buttered Scones

The excitement of two dwarves visiting has not even begun to die down when the bell rings once more. It's two more dwarves. Your feelings of dread, it seems, were well justified.

The four dwarves sit and talk of dwarf things like dragons and gold when the bell starts ringing like it's about to be ripped from its chain. Four, no five, more dwarves have arrived. This is certainly turning out to be a party no one could anticipate.

There's nine visitors now and they all begin to shout out their orders for food and drink. Some ask for ale and some for porter. One of them even wants coffee, which you will now have to brew special. And, of course, all of them are asking for more tea-cakes. You hurry about trying to be the best host you can be. You set the jug of coffee out for them. You realize all of your cakes have now been eaten up, but your guests are still ravenous. Time to start them on a round of buttered scones.

Hurry, there's yet another guest at the door!

Buttered Scones
(one dozen)

2 cups flour
1 tablespoon baking powder
2 tablespoons sugar
½ teaspoon salt
3 tablespoons butter
1 egg
¾ cup milk

Mix the dry ingredients together in a bowl. Cut in the butter until the mixture resembles course crumbs. Beat, then add the egg.

Turn the mixture onto a floured board and knead lightly. Roll out the dough to ¾ inch thickness and cut with a 2 inch cookie cutter.

Place the scones about an inch apart on a lightly greased baking sheet. Brush the tops with a little beaten egg or milk. Bake in a preheated 450° oven for about 10 to 15 minutes, or until golden brown. Serve warm – with butter of course!

Raspberry Jam and Apple Tart
Mince Pie and Cheese
Pork Pie and Salad
A Few Eggs for Wisdom
Cold Poached Chicken and Pickles

This time it's a loud knock instead of a ring. It sounds like someone is banging and denting your beautiful door with a stick!

It's more dwarves, four more of them! And there is the wizard at last, standing behind them and laughing. Is he going to pay for the damage to your door?

Of course they are all hungry. What follows is an astounding barrage of food orders the like of which has never been seen before or since:
Tea, red wine, raspberry jam and apple tart, mince-pies and cheese, pork-pie and salad, more cakes and ale, coffee, eggs, and your cold chicken and pickles. How did he know I even had that, you wonder? This wizard seems to know your pantry remarkably well.

Raspberry Jam

4 cups sugar
4 cups raspberries

Place the berries in a large saucepan. Bring them to a boil over high heat, mashing the berries as they cook. Boil for one minute, stirring constantly.
Add the sugar, return to a boil, then boil until the mixture gels (coats the back of a spoon). This will take approximately five minutes.

Ladle into sterilized canning jars, filling them to within ¼-inch of the top. Place the lid on, then tighten the ring. Submerge the jars in a large pot of boiling water.
Make sure to keep the jars covered with at least 2 inches of water. Boil them for 5 to 10 minutes.

Our family has a long history of making our own jam. It is really not very difficult and can be especially rewarding if you have picked the berries yourself.

Apple Tart

1 and ½ cups flour
dash salt
1 and ½ sticks (6 ounces) cold unsalted butter
2 tablespoons melted butter
one third cup ice water
3 tablespoons sugar
1 tablespoon flour
4 large apples, peeled and cut into ¼ inch thick slices

Sift together the flour and salt. Add the cold butter and work it in just until the butter is the size of peas. Sprinkle the ice water over the mixture and combine. Transfer the dough to a lightly floured surface and knead two or three times. Form the dough into a disk. Roll the dough into a 16 inch round about ¼ inch thick. Place the dough onto a large baking sheet lined with parchment paper.

In a small bowl, combine 2 tablespoons of the sugar with one tablespoon of flour and sprinkle over the dough. Arrange the apple slices on top in overlapping circles to within 3 inches of the edge. Fold the dough over the apples at the edges. Brush the apples with the melted butter and sprinkle with the remaining 1 and ½ tablespoons of sugar.

Preheat the oven to 400°. Bake the tart in the center of the oven for 1 hour, or until the apples are tender and golden, and the crust is deeply golden in color.

Mince Pie and Cheese
(With this flavorful pie, I would likely serve a simple, creamy, farmhouse cheddar)

The Mincemeat

3 cups raisins
1 and ½ cups currants
1 cup dried cherries
½ cup dark rum or brandy
2 medium apples, peeled, cored and chopped finely
½ teaspoon ground cinnamon
½ teaspoon ground allspice
½ teaspoon freshly ground nutmeg
½ teaspoon ground cloves
¼ cup chopped roasted hazelnuts
1 cup brown sugar
4 tablespoons hot water
2 tablespoons butter

Place raisins, currants, and dried cherries into a large bowl. Add rum, mix well, cover and let sit covered in a cool place for a day, stirring occasionally. Blanch the chopped apple in boiling water. Drain the apples and add them to the soaked fruit, along with the mixed spices and chopped roasted hazelnuts. Heat the water, brown sugar, and butter, stirring constantly, until the sugar melts. Add this to the fruit mixture and, again, mix thoroughly. Your mincemeat may be used immediately or may be stored in sterilized canning jars, as we did with the raspberry jam.

The Crust (pâte brisée)

1 and ¼ cups flour
½ teaspoon salt
1 tablespoon granulated sugar
½ cup unsalted butter, chilled, and cut into ½ inch pieces
¼ cup (approximately) ice water

Sift together the flour and salt. Add the cold butter and work it in just until the butter is the size of peas. Sprinkle the ice water over the mixture and combine. Transfer the dough to a lightly floured surface and knead 2 or 3 times. Form the dough into a disk.   Chill the dough for an hour before rolling. Roll the dough into two rounds: one 10 inch and one 9 inch, both about ¼ inch thick. Place the larger dough into a pie pan. Fill the pie, then top with the smaller dough, then crimp the two together. Bake at 375 degrees for one hour or until nicely browned.

Pork Pie and Salad

The Pie

1 recipe short-crust pastry (see mince pie above)
1 pound lean pork
4 ounces bacon
2 tablespoons flour, seasoned with salt and a dash of garlic powder
(feel free to add other herbs and spices that you might like with the dish)
2 tablespoons chopped, fresh sage
1 large onion, sliced
salt and pepper

Cut the pork and bacon into cubes and roll them in the seasoned flour. Brown the pork, bacon and onion, then add water to cover. Bring to the boil and simmer for 1 and a half to 2 hours until the meat is cooked.

Roll out the pastry and line a pie dish with one crust. Drain the meat and put it in the pie pan with the chopped sage, salt, and pepper. Moisten with two tablespoons of the stock left from cooking the meat.

Cover with the top crust and bake for thirty to thirty five minutes at 400 degrees.

The Salad

Basic Red Wine Vinaigrette

3 tablespoons good red wine vinegar
3 tablespoons nice extra virgin olive oil
1 clove garlic, finely minced
dash salt and pepper
2 tablespoons fresh herbs
(basil and parsley mixed or 1 tablespoon fresh thyme)
1 teaspoon dry mustard (optional)

Place all the ingredients except for the oil in a bowl. Whisk in the oil until it emulsifies.

I would serve this over fresh lettuce, sliced mushrooms, and tomatoes – hopefully from your own garden!

A Few Eggs for Wisdom

Here is a good recipe for poached eggs.

Fill a frying pan or saucepan with 2 inches of water. Bring the water to a simmer (never let it boil!). You can place a dash of white vinegar in the water to help the eggs coagulate. Carefully crack the egg into the water. Don't cook too many at once (no more than 3 or 4). When the whites are set and the yolk is done to your liking, lift them out with a slotted spoon, (and if you want to be fancy) cut off the ruff edges, then pat them dry with a paper towel.

Cold Poached Chicken and Pickles

4 skinless and boneless chicken breasts
1 and one half cups water
1 cup diced onion
½ cup dry white wine
2 sliced carrots
2 stalks sliced celery
½ teaspoon fresh ground pepper
2 tablespoons fresh coarsely chopped parsley
1 teaspoon fresh thyme leafs
1 bay leaf

Place chicken in a large saucepan. Add all the other ingredients, and bring to a boil. Reduce heat and simmer uncovered for five minutes or until chicken is done. Remove the pan from the heat and let it sit uncovered for 30 minutes. Place the chicken and poaching liquid in a large bowl. Cover and chill.

Serve with…

Dill Pickles

one and a half to two pounds small cucumbers
(you can cut them in half to speed the process)
2 cups cold water
½ teaspoon celery seed
3 tablespoons sea salt
1 tablespoon dill seed
2 tablespoons fresh chopped dill
2 cups white vinegar
1 tablespoon sugar
4 cloves sliced fresh garlic
1 teaspoon mustard seed
½ teaspoon red-pepper flakes

Divide the cucumbers into four pint-sized jars. In a large bowl mix together all of the other ingredients. Funnel the mixture to fill each jar. Cap tightly and refrigerate at least one week before serving. We often re-use this pickling liquid once or twice.

Fireside Shortbread Biscuits

Things have finally quieted down a little. You sit by the fire chewing on a biscuit. You've somehow managed to lose your appetite in all of the commotion. Yes, the dwarves have helped serve and tidy a bit, but they've also eaten up most of your food, and they're showing no signs of wanting to leave. What if they stay the night and expect breakfast tomorrow morning? You certainly don't have eggs enough for 14 guests.

Fireside Shortbread Biscuits

1 and ¾ cups flour
1 stick unsalted butter (room temperature)
two thirds cup fine sugar

Preheat oven to 350 degrees.
In a large bowl cream together the butter and sugar until light and fluffy. Sift the flour into the butter and sugar and mix until incorporated.

Lightly dust your counter with flour and roll out the dough to ½ inch thick. Mark the surface all over with a fork. Cut into rectangles or rounds.

Place the shortbreads on a lightly greased baking sheet and bake for 25 minutes, or until pale brown and crisp.

Sprinkle the warm shortbreads with fine sugar and leave to cool on a rack.

Fried Eggs and Ham for a Dwarf

Of course they're staying the night, and here come the breakfast orders. Well, you suppose you might be able to manage a first breakfast, but a second is entirely out of the question. They did say some interesting things about dragons and treasure, and the wizard did vouch for you, but they expect you to be some sort of thief. Completely out of the question, you think. Then again, you can't deny the rush of excitement you felt hearing about secret doors and treasure maps. You could use a little excitement in your life, couldn't you? Maybe things will make more sense after a good night's sleep.

Fried Eggs and Ham for a Dwarf

Fried Ham Slices

2 slices center-cut ham (¼ inch thick)
1 teaspoon butter
2 teaspoons brown sugar (optional)

Trim the rind from the ham slices. Melt the butter in a large, heavy skillet. Sprinkle the slices with brown sugar if desired. Place them in the skillet and fry over medium heat until golden brown on each side (about three minutes per side). Remove the slices to a platter.

Turn heat to low. Break the eggs gently into the hot fat left in the pan (making sure not to break the yolks!). With a spoon, dip some of the boiling fat over the top of the eggs while they are cooking. Fry slowly until the whites are completely set and the yolks begin to thicken, but are not hard.

Beverages from a highly unanticipated celebration

Tea, of course, considering the first guests arrived at tea time. Then you served a little beer, along with some ale and porter.

Of course some always want coffee. Why can't they just enjoy tea like a civilized person?

Then the fanciest of them all got some of your best red wine.

You make and often enjoy a wide variety of beers, including: ales, porters, and stouts. You are perhaps most fond of ale. You always keep a barrel of ale in your cellar.

The wine you served them was aged almost 50 years. It was kept for the most special of occasions. You wonder if this little soiree was worth the bottle. Although the wine wasn't called this at the time, one day it will come to be known as a 'Cabernet.' Such a strange and fanciful appellation, much like 'soiree.'

Roasted Mutton on Skewers

By now your journey is well underway. After waking up late, you ran off after the dwarves. Why did you do that? You forgot... pretty much everything. You've been slung atop a pony and dragged so very far from home to uncivilized lands. You've been chilled to the bone and rained upon. You're exhausted. You don't even have anything with which to blow your nose. And now, in the darkest part of the night, you have stumbled across three trolls! They are the largest and most foul creatures you have ever seen, and you have been sent to spy on them. But that's not all. For some reason you have decided to try and pick one of their pockets. Definitely not your brightest moment.

The trolls are roasting mutton on long wooden spits and licking the gravy from their hands. They are also drinking from massive jugs that probably contain ale. Hmm, that mutton sure does smell good. Maybe they won't notice you at all.

Roasted Mutton on Skewers

2 pounds leg of lamb or mutton
1 pint of ale
2 onions sliced
1 teaspoon salt
½ teaspoon pepper
4 or 5 sprigs of fresh thyme
1 smashed clove of garlic
1 tablespoon melted butter

Slice the mutton into thin strips or cubes about ½ inch thick. Place all of the other ingredients in a bowl. Marinate the mutton for several hours in the liquid. Skewer the mutton slices and onions with long spits. Roast over a campfire or hot coals.

Fire Toasted Bacon

The trolls have been dispatched - turned to stone - thanks in no small part to your brave (and foolish) efforts. You've discovered their larder and treasury and recovered some very interesting items from both. Right now the food is more exciting than the treasure. Taking inventory you find: bread, cheese, ale, and bacon. That would be even better than mutton when toasted in the embers of a cheerful fire.

Fire Toasted Bacon
(with bread, cheese, and ale)

2 pounds thick cut, smoked, cured, bacon with the rind attached.

Cut bacon into four inch by two inch chunks and notch the sides a few times about ½ inch deep. Skewer the bacon. Hold it over the top of your campfire until it starts to sizzle. Keep rotating the bacon slowly over the campfire embers until it is heavily dripping. When crispy outside and cooked through, slide the bacon off the skewer, using a slice of bread as a sort of mitt and plate combined.

Serve with cheese and ale. I think a Cheshire or cheddar would be appropriate.

During your time with the elves

Visiting with elves tends to make you forget all of the discomforts of the trip getting to them. Unfortunately it also makes you forget all of the wonderful food and drink you enjoyed during your visit. As you think back to your stay in the elven valley you can't now remember a single thing that you ate or drank. You know that you had a wonderful and restful time, but the specifics are more than a little hazy.

Under-Mountain

Now you've really gotten yourself into it. You find yourself lost far underground in the heart of a mountain. The caves go on for miles twisting and turning. It feels like you will never find your way out. The only things keeping you going are fond memories of sunshine and wind, and your favorite foods of course. What are your favorite foods as a representative halfling? Bacon and eggs has to be near the top of the list. We've seen that recipe before, except with ham. Mushrooms, as we will find a little way down the road, are a leading candidate, as is freshly baked bread with butter or cheese.

Near the Summit

Finally free from the mountain you now find yourself on a ledge, having been carried to the top of the mountain by an eagle! Before this you managed to nibble a bit of sorrel, and drink from a small mountain-stream. You also ate three wild strawberries. What a feast!

Later the eagles brought you and the dwarves rabbits, hares, and a small sheep. The dwarves roasted these over an open fire, though you would have preferred a nice loaf of bread with butter, over more meat toasted on sticks. The cooking manner for the rabbits and sheep would be the same as for the fire toasted bacon from the earlier chapter.

Herbs such as thyme, sage, and marjoram are very important in halfling cookery. It's a shame the eagles didn't bring you any of these, or at least a bit of salt.

Eating with Bears
Fresh Bread with Butter, Honey and Clotted Cream

You have finally gotten yourself someplace nice to rest and to refill your empty stomach. Does this enormous but kindly man actually think you are a rabbit? Nah, he has to be joking, you hope.

You sit with the dwarves, and the wizard, and the enormous man with his marvelous animal friends. You drink many bowls of mead. You eat bread with butter, honey, and clotted cream. You eat enough of it to stuff a sofa.

Fresh Bread with Butter, Honey and Clotted Cream

1 cup warm water
1 cup slightly warm buttermilk
¼ cup melted butter (cooled)
6 cups bread flour
½ cup honey
2 large eggs, beaten
1 tablespoon salt
4 teaspoons yeast

Mix together your water, butter, and buttermilk. Add 2 cups of the flour and mix until smooth. Add the honey, salt, yeast, and eggs. Stir together until smooth. Allow the dough to sit uncovered for 15 minutes. Begin to add the rest of the flour ½ cup at a time. Stir until the dough becomes too hard to mix. Continue to slowly add the remaining flour until the dough is still barely sticky. Knead the dough until smooth (about ten minutes).

Place the dough into a lightly greased bowl. Cover the bowl with a cloth and set aside in a warm place for about an hour. Scrape the dough out onto a lightly floured surface. Cut it in half. Shape it into two ovals the length of a 5x9 inch loaf pan. Roll the dough, being sure to lightly press with each rotation. Pinch the seam closed with your fingers. Place into two greased 5x9 loaf pans. You can also cook them freeform on a baking sheet. Cover with towels and allow to rise until double in size (about one hour).

Brush the tops of the loaves with egg wash. Bake in a 375

degree oven for 30-35 minutes. The bread is done when you tap on the bottom of the loaf and it sounds hollow. Remove from the pans and cool on a wire rack.

Serve with butter, honey, and clotted cream!

Twice-Baked Honey-Cakes

Sadly the time comes soon enough to leave the house of the enormous but kindly man. You are headed into the largest and darkest forest in the world. These dwarves seem determined to visit all of the very worst places. You would much rather stay at the edge of the wood in his strange yet comfortable home. Fortunately this bear-like fellow has provided you with plenty of supplies for your trip: nuts, flour, jars of dried fruits, earthenware pots of honey, and twice-baked cakes that will keep good a long time. He certainly was tight-lipped about the recipe for those honey-cakes. They have plenty of honey in them, though, that much you can smell for certain.

Twice-Baked Honey-Cakes

1 cup sugar
4 tablespoons melted butter, cooled
4 eggs
1 cup strong coffee (cooled)
1 cup honey
3 cups flour
2 teaspoons baking powder
1 teaspoon baking soda
1 tablespoon cinnamon
1 and ½ cups raisins and or other dried fruit
¼ cup slivered almonds

Whisk together the coffee, butter, and honey. Add the dry ingredients and beat until incorporated. Stir in the dried fruit and nuts. Pour your batter into a 9 by 13 inch pan. Bake for one hour at 325 degrees, or until a toothpick comes out clean. Cut the cake into thick slices and return them to the oven to bake a second time for 10 to 15 minutes more.

More lean days followed by a feast

Through the forest you go. And though you were given a good supply of food for your journey it is already fast running out. You try to shoot some game (well, squirrels) but it tastes too awful to eat. You have become hopelessly lost.

After a nasty incident with some rather large spiders you are lured by the smell of food. There are elves in the woods and they are having some sort of party. You try to sneak up on it but just can't seem to find them. Eventually, and perhaps thankfully, you are captured by the elves. Aren't they supposed to be friendly? Oh, these elves don't like dwarves. Great.

Elf prison isn't so bad really. Especially when you can make yourself... very difficult to see. You dream of eggs and bacon, and toast and butter. And you steal a pie and a bottle of wine. Eventually you'll have to figure out some way to free these dwarves. Maybe shove them into barrels?

Believe it or not the barrel idea worked! Unfortunately you've caught a terrible cold during the ride down the river. You're given a lovely welcoming feast when you arrive at the town by the lake, but you are so sick you don't remember a single thing you ate.

Traveler's Bread

The lake guys sure are cheap. This 'traveler's' bread they gave you is the worst cracker or bread you've ever eaten. It's getting so hard you'll need diamonds on your teeth to be able to chew through it. Your dreams will forever be filled with eggs and bacon, until you get back to your cozy little home, where you can cook to your heart's content.

To make the 'traveler's' bread a little more interesting, you might try adding milk instead of half of the water. You might also replace some of the flour with cornmeal and or add some honey.

The best advice is to avoid it entirely and bring the twice-baked honey cakes instead, or the elvish version if you can find the recipe.

Did someone say something about a dragon? Oh, I suppose they want you to go down there and talk to it. What could go wrong?

Traveler's Bread

2 cups flour
¾ cup water
1 tablespoon lard or vegetable oil
1 teaspoon salt

Mix the ingredients together, knead several times, and spread the dough out ½ inch thick on a non-greased cookie sheet. Bake for 30 minutes at 400 degrees. Remove from the oven, cut the dough into 3-inch squares, press patterns of holes (not all the way through) into the dough with a fork. Turn the dough over, and return to the oven to bake for another half hour. Turn the oven off and leave the door closed. Leave the bread in the oven until it is cool.

Part 2. Recipes from the tales of The Halfling's nephew

You are a much younger halfling now, and this is your story. It's much more serious, yet there is still time for the important things like breakfast, tea, and supper. In fact you'll take six meals a day whenever possible!

Your story begins with a party. Hey, nothing wrong with that. Unlike the last time, this celebration has been anticipated for a very long while. It's a birthday party for you and your uncle. The day was filled with eating and the night with fireworks. And then... well then you lost your uncle to the elves. Will you ever see him again?

Now many years have passed and it's your birthday once more. You celebrate with a last glass of the good wine. Then it is finally time for your adventure to begin.

Where is that wizard? Is he always late?

Fair White Bread of the Elves

Someone or something is after you. Luckily you run into a group of elves. They keep you safe and feed you well, including the best apples anyone has ever eaten.

Aside from the apples you are treated to the finest bread you have ever tasted, fruits as sweet as wild berries, and a fragrant drink, both cool and golden.

The drink comes from the purest spring in the elven valley and smells of honey and mountain flowers. It refreshes you from your weariness and fright.

Fair White Bread of the Elves

2 and ½ cups warm water
one package dry yeast
1 tablespoon sugar
6 cups flour
½ tablespoon salt
4 tablespoons softened butter

Combine the water with the yeast and sugar in a large bowl and let stand about ten minutes. Add 5 cups of flour and the salt to the yeast mixture. Stir together, adding the remaining flour slowly, until the dough pulls cleanly away from the sides of the bowl. Knead in the butter until the dough is smooth and not sticky.

Turn the dough out onto a lightly floured surface and continue kneading until it is smooth and elastic. Shape the dough into a ball and place it in a large, lightly buttered bowl to rise until doubled in volume.

Place the dough on a lightly floured surface and divide in two equal portions. Working with one piece at a time, roll the dough out into a 9 inch wide by 12 inch tall rectangle. Fold one third of the dough down, then fold it down again. Pinch the bottom seam to seal. Your rectangle should be approximately 9 by 4 inches now. Turn the side with the seam up. Fold each end over about one half inch, tuck in any loose ends and pinch to seal. Place the loaf seam side down into a buttered 8 by 4 inch loaf pan.

Allow the dough to rise in the pans until they double in volume. It will rise above the top of the pan.

Preheat your oven to 375 degrees.

Place the loaves in your oven and bake for 35-40 minutes. When done, the loaves will be golden in color and will sound hollow when tapped.

Remove the loaves from the pans and let them cool completely on a wire rack.

Serve with fresh berries and Elvish Draught.

Elvish Draught

One pint of Spring Water
1 teaspoon wildflower honey
1 teaspoon clover honey
2 or 3 drops of anise oil (optional)

Stir the ingredients together, then shake until completely dissolved and lightly golden and yet still clear in color. The spring water should be lightly carbonated.

Farmer's Mushrooms

You're chased once again by those horrible tall shadows on horseback, and you're saved once again - this time by an old friend. Well, perhaps friend is a little strong. You have history with this good farmer, and more specifically, you have a history with his vicious dogs.

The farmer's wife greets you with a big jug of beer that's as good as any from one of your favorite inns. She also carries a basket. This seems most promising. The scent of cooked mushrooms rises from underneath its cover.

You sit down to dinner with the farmer and his family. There's plenty of beer, a massive dish of mushrooms and bacon, and other delicious farmhouse cuisine. Even the dogs feast on rinds and cracked bones.

Farmer's Mushrooms

one pound mushrooms
4 strips of bacon
dash of salt and pepper
½ teaspoon fresh thyme leaves
juice of ½ lemon
1 tablespoon butter

Slice your mushrooms not too thin or thick. You can use white button mushrooms (crimini). You can also mix in some wild mushrooms such as porcini, morels, or chanterelles. Slice your bacon into smallish pieces. Sauté for a couple minutes in the butter. Add the rest of the ingredients except the lemon juice and cook for several minutes until the bacon is crisp and the mushrooms are tender. Sprinkle with lemon juice. Enjoy!

White Bread in the House of the Ancients

Lost again. This time in the most ancient of forests. The trees are out to get you. You swear you saw one of them move to block your path. And now you are rescued once more. This time the hero is at once the silliest and most serious person you have ever met. His clothing is colorful, his wife beautiful, and his house the epitome of comfort and safety.

You stay for a while with him and he feeds you several meals. You remember white bread, yellow cream, honeycomb, butter, milk, cheese, green herbs, and ripe berries. Could a halfling ever ask for more?

There was also a drink that was as clear as water but behaved more like strong wine. You were sad to leave the safe house behind, but your journey always calls.

White Bread in the House of the Ancients

5 and ½ to 6 cups flour
3 tablespoons sugar or honey
2 envelopes yeast
2 teaspoons salt
1 and ½ cups water
½ cup milk
2 tablespoons unsalted butter

In a large bowl, combine 2 cups flour, sugar or honey, yeast, and salt. Heat the water, milk, and butter until warm, then beat into the flour mixture. Stir in enough remaining flour to make a soft dough. Knead on a lightly floured surface until smooth and elastic (about 8 to 10 minutes). Let the dough rest 10 minutes.
Divide dough in half. Roll each half into a 12 x 6 inch rectangle. Beginning at the short end of the rectangle, roll up tightly as for a jelly roll. Pinch the seams and ends to seal. Place, seam side down, in greased loaf pans. Cover, and let rise in a warm place until doubled in size.

Bake at 400°F for 25 to 30 minutes.
Let the bread cool a little before eating (if possible).

Serve with butter, milk, cheese, green herbs, and ripe berries.

Mock Yellow (Devonshire) Cream

3 ounces softened cream cheese
1 teaspoon powdered sugar
1 cup heavy cream
Beat the cream cheese and sugar until fluffy. Gradually add the cream and beat until thickened. Cover and refrigerate overnight before serving.

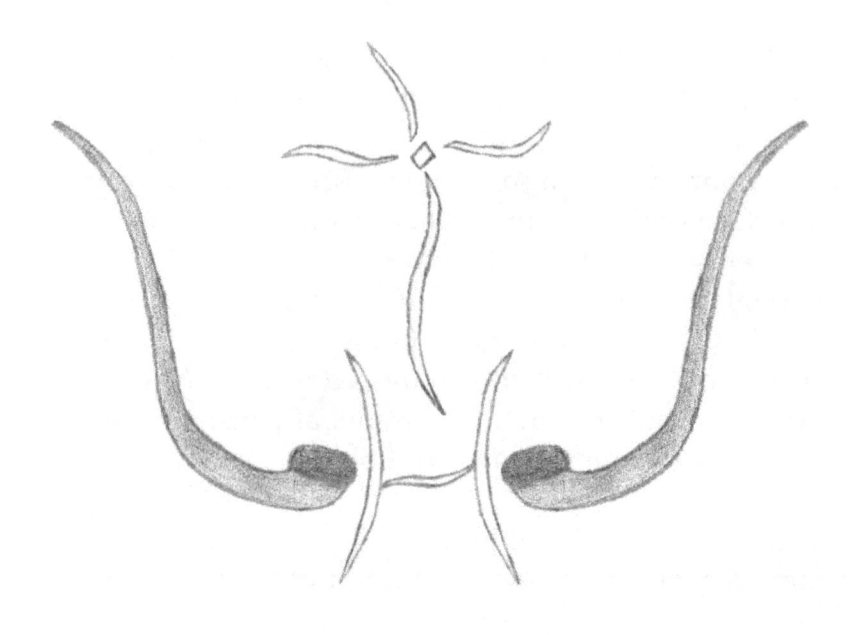

**Blackberry Tart and Pea Soup at the Inn
served with a lovely Rustic Bread**

After an awful ordeal with some sort of barrow ghosts you have finally arrived at the famous town where halflings and humans live together in peace. The innkeeper sure is a friendly fellow, even if he does seem a bit confused.

Luckily there are rooms available to fit your size. But before bed we must sample the local fare!

There is hot soup, cold meats, a blackberry tart, loaves of rustic bread, butter, and ripe cheese, as well as some excellent beer.

Blackberry Tart

2 cups flour
¼ cup sugar
Pinch of salt
1 and ½ sticks cold unsalted butter
2 egg yolks
3 tablespoons cold water

5 cups blackberries
¾ cup sugar
¼ cup flour
2 tablespoons unsalted butter
1 large egg yolk
1 tablespoon water
2 tablespoons sugar

Combine the flour, sugar, and salt. Add the butter and work with your fingertips until the mixture resembles small peas. Add the egg yolks and water until the dough comes together. Place the dough onto a work surface, knead two or three times and shape into a disk. Wrap the dough and refrigerate until chilled.

On a lightly floured surface, roll out two-thirds of the dough to a twelve inch round. Transfer it to a 9-inch tart pan 1 inch deep. Press the dough into the pan, folding in the overhanging dough to the sides. Trim the overhang and knead the scraps into the remaining dough.
On a floured surface, roll out the remaining dough to a ten inch round. Cut the round into inch-wide strips.

In a large bowl, toss the blackberries, sugar and flour.

Spoon the mixture into the tart shell. Scatter the butter on top. Arrange the dough strips over the berries in a lattice shape, pressing the ends into the edges of the tart. Brush the lattice with the egg yolk and water mixture; sprinkle with two tablespoons of sugar.

Bake the tart for about one hour at 350°, or until the pastry is golden and the juices are bubbling. Transfer to a wire rack to cool.

Pea Soup at the Inn

2 cups dried split peas
6 cups vegetable stock
½ cup sliced carrot
½ cup sliced celery
1 tablespoon butter
1 cup diced onion
1 clove garlic, minced
2 teaspoons salt
1 teaspoon pepper
½ teaspoon dried thyme
1 teaspoon fresh chives for garnish
2 green onions, finely sliced
1 teaspoon finely chopped fresh tarragon

Saute the onions, carrot and celery briefly in the butter. Add the peas, garlic, salt, pepper, and thyme. Add the vegetable stock and simmer gently for one and a half to two hours. Garnish with chives and tarragon. Note, if you prefer firmer carrots, add them in the last 20 minutes.

The Stock
1 large-ish onion
8 large white mushrooms
1 large carrot
1 stalk celery
4 cloves garlic
¼ cup fresh parsley
2 tablespoons butter
½ cup dry white wine
water to more than cover the vegetables (about 8 cups)

1 teaspoon salt
½ teaspoon freshly ground pepper

Saute the onion in the butter. Add the rest of the vegetables, coarsely chopped. Saute for a couple minutes. Add the wine and bring to a boil. Add the water until the vegetables are more than covered. Simmer for about 20 minutes or until you realize it "smells very good." Strain the stock into another pot and set it aside.

Rustic Bread

The Sponge
1 tablespoon active dry yeast
1 cup warm water
1 cup flour

The Dough
4 cups white flour
1 cup whole wheat flour
1 and ¼ cup warm water
1 tablespoon honey
1 teaspoon salt

Dissolve the yeast in the warm water then add the flour. Let it all rest for at least one hour.

In a large bowl, combine the sponge, 2 cups of flour, water, and honey. Add the salt and remaining flour, stirring in about ½ cup at a time, until the dough comes together. Turn onto a lightly floured surface and knead about five minutes. Place in a lightly greased bowl to rise until doubled.

Turn the dough onto a lightly floured surface and gently deflate. Shape into a ball and place on a baking sheet. Sprinkle flour over the top of the loaf and cover with a dish towel. Let the dough rise for about an hour.

Bake for 35 to 40 minutes at 450°, or until the crust is dark brown.

You can add a small pan of water to the bottom rack of

your oven, below the bread, to create steam while the bread cooks. This will make an even better crust.

The Bread of the Elves

Your journey has gone on and on, over and under mountains, through bogs and forests. There have been sadly very few good meals along the way.

You were given some apples by the halflings at the inn. You had two different elvish draughts. One of them was clear in color and had no taste, but made you feel much stronger. The other was the official liquor of the elvish valley. This one was warm and fragrant and also made you feel stronger, as well as more awake.

Your traveling food consisted mostly of stale bread and dried fruits.

When you arrived at the elvish valley you met your dear uncle again! There was a great feast in celebration, however you do not recall now what was served. And even though you stayed for two months in the valley you did not record any of your meals.

Finally, after the most perilous of journeys, you arrived at the elvish forest kingdom. There you stayed and rested for a good long while. When they sent you on your way they gave you some of their famous elvish traveling bread. It's more a cake than a bread: light brown on the outside and cream-colored on the inside. Many feel it is even superior to the twice-baked honey cakes. They keep fresh for many days if kept in their wrappings.

The Bread of the Elves

3 eggs well beaten, until light yellow in color
½ cup wildflower or orange honey
2 tablespoons orange juice
one eighth cup finely pulverized Brazil nuts or macadamias
¼ cup melted unsalted butter
2 cups fine cornmeal
¼ cup flour
¼ teaspoon salt

Add the honey to the beaten eggs, along with the orange juice, butter, and nuts. Gradually fold in all of the dry ingredients. Bake on a cookie sheet or in a madeleine pan at 375 degrees for 15 minutes, until light brown on the outside. If you want the cakes to be uniform, you could use a mold or cookie cutters as you bake them. I feel that the thickness of a thin madeleine is correct for this bread, regardless of whether you use a mold.

Your friends have their own food-related adventures

The other two halflings suffer through a terrible captivity by goblins. They are carried like parcels for many miles. They are forced to drink some goblin liquor (which does refresh their strength and ease their pain). The only food they are offered is some gray bread and some unnamed dried flesh (which they did not eat). Luckily they also still had a few pieces of the elvish traveling bread.

When they were rescued by the tree-men they were treated to some of their wondrous draughts which completely refresh and invigorate. Is it your imagination or have your friends grown a little since you saw them last?

Then they had a lovely feast with their friends in the ruins of the evil wizard's city. There was toast made from slightly stale bread, wine, beer, salted pork, bacon, butter, and honey. The main recipe here would be basically the same as the fire-toasted bacon we saw earlier.

A Pair of Young Coneys

The story now returns to you. Alongside the farmer's mushrooms, your next meal is perhaps the most beloved and famous. It also shows the importance of a caring meal even, and perhaps most especially, during the darkest times.

You find yourself with your best friend and an odd shriveled sort of creature in a lush and fragrant land, which happens to sit right next to the most evil land (where sadly you are now headed). The creature has caught two young rabbits and now your best friend wants to cook them in a sort of stew.

He wishes he had turnips, carrots and taters (potatoes). He wishes he could make fish and chips. He wishes he had some stock and onions. But all he has is a few herbs and the rabbits, so he does the very best he can.

You enjoy the stew together, along with some of the elvish traveling bread. It seems like a feast.

A Pair of Young Coneys

2 young rabbits, skinned and cut up
A few bay-leaves, some thyme and sage
(about ¼ cup herbs tied into a bunch)
4 cups water
1 teaspoon salt

In a shallow pan (such as a high sided frying pan), brown the coneys using fat from the skin. Add the water, herbs, and salt. Bring to a simmer and stew for close on an hour.

Serve with ½ piece of elf bread.

A few last bites

Rescued again. This time by a group of tall and proud men. They seem like good and honorable friends. They take you to their secret hideout and serve you dinner.

There is a cask of pale yellow wine, bread and butter, salted meats, dried fruits, and good red cheese. You enjoy three helpings.

During the last leg of your journey, before entering the evil place, you eat the dried fruits, bread, and salted meat the men gave you.

Finally you have your last meal before going down into the evil place. You fear it might be the last meal you ever share with your best friend. You have some of the food the men gave you, and some of the elvish bread, with just a sip of water.

White Cakes of the Kings
and Fine White Bread of Kings

The tale returns once again to your friends: the other two halflings. Here you are in the greatest city of men. It is higher and more glorious than you ever could have imagined. And you thought your family home was too grand.

A young friend takes you on a tour of the city and feeds you the types of things the soldiers regularly eat. There is bread and butter, cheese and apples, and a flagon of ale, served on wooden plates and cups.

Later you have an audience with the somewhat creepy ruler of the city. Here you are served fancy white cakes on silver plates with silver flagons and cups.

Much later, the city is under siege by goblins and evil men. Your typical meal now consists of a small loaf of bread and a small pat of butter, with a cup of thin milk. You wish you were back home.

You watch as the ruler's son eats some nice white bread and has a drink of wine. Unfortunately for him, he also has to sit beside his father.

White Cakes of the Kings

12 tablespoons softened unsalted butter
1 and ½ cups sugar
2 cups flour
2 teaspoons baking powder
dash of salt
6 egg whites beaten
¾ cup milk
2 teaspoons vanilla

Butter the bottom of two 9-inch round pans.

Beat the butter and sugar in a large bowl until light and fluffy. Mix together the flour, baking powder, and salt. Combine the egg whites, milk and vanilla. Slowly mix all wet ingredients into the dry, being careful not to overwork. Pour the batter into your pans and smooth the top. Bake for about 25 to 30 minutes at 350 degrees, or until a toothpick inserted in the center comes out clean.

Cool the cakes in the pans briefly, then turn them out onto a rack and let cool completely.

Fine White Bread of Kings

2 teaspoons yeast
½ cup warm water
1 cup milk or buttermilk
4 cups flour
4 ounces unsalted softened butter
½ teaspoon salt
¼ cup water at room temperature

Stir together yeast and warm water in a small bowl. Combine the flour and salt in a large bowl. Add the butter. While mixing, add enough of the room temperature water to make a smooth, elastic dough. Cover and allow to rise in a cool place until doubled in size.

Shape to fit a rectangular loaf pan. Cover and allow to rise again until doubled.

Preheat your oven to 375 degrees. Score the top of the loaf diagonally 3 times with a very sharp knife (of Elvish craft preferably). Place the loaf pan in the center of the preheated oven and bake for 50 minutes.

A few last bites (I mean it this time)

You are really in trouble now. You have entered the evil land. You've been captured by goblins, had some horrible burning drink poured down your throat, finally escaped the goblins, are now disguised as goblins, and are heading for the volcano to complete your quest. The only thing keeping you going is the elvish bread, a little water, and the last of the dried fruit the nice man gave you so long ago.

It is really the elven bread that is keeping you going. You would have failed long ago without it, and your supply is fast running out. The bread gives you strength unlike any other food can possibly give. You may have enough left to get you to the end, but certainly not enough to make it back home.

Now your quest is fulfilled. You have been rescued by eagles from the flowing lava and are now sitting with the king at a great victory feast. You do not recall any of the foods you ate there.

And now you are almost home. You stop at the inn where much of your journey began. The befuddled innkeeper is still there and still cheerful. The supper and the beer are much the same as they were on your first visit. You take great comfort in this. It seems the world is going to be all right after all.

About the Author:

Vanessa Kittle is a former chef, soldier, and lawyer who now teaches English. Her fantasy and science fiction stories have been featured by Akashic Books. Vanessa has also recently appeared in magazines such as the Rhysling Anthology, Contemporary American Voices, Dreams and Nightmares, Abyss and Apex, Star*Line, and Silver Blade.

Her books have received hundreds of thousands of downloads on Amazon in the genres of fantasy, science fiction, paranormal romance, and cooking.

Vanessa edits the Abramelin Poetry Journal. She enjoys watching cheesy movies, cooking, and gardening.

Try Vanessa's new epic fantasy series
The School for Humans on Amazon.

CPSIA information can be obtained
at www.ICGtesting.com
Printed in the USA
LVHW111708220620
658705LV00003B/1012